'Lenten Prayers

FOR

Seniors

DENNIS H. FERENCE

Liguori

ONE LIGUORI DRIVE
LIGUORI MO 63057-9999

Imprimi Potest:
Richard Thibodeau, C.Ss.R.
Provincial, Denver Province
The Redemptorists

© 2000, Liguori Publications
ISBN 0-7648-0611-4
Printed in the United States of America
03 04   5 4 3 2

Scripture quotations are from the *New Revised Standard Version of the Bible*, copyright © 1989 by the Division of Christian Education of the National Council of Churches of Christ in the USA. Used with permission. All rights reserved.

To order, call 1-800-325-9521
www.liguori.org
www.catholicbooksonline.com

Cover design by Wendy Barnes

Preface

∾

I have always thought of the Lenten season as a very special time. Even as a young boy I greeted Ash Wednesday enthusiastically as the beginning of a wonderful opportunity to get closer to God.

In those early days of youth I measured the success of Lent by how faithfully I kept my Lenten resolution to give up one thing or another and by how many times I attended Mass and said the rosary. And with my sacrifice and my efforts at prayer often came a heightened sense of communication and friendship with God that gave each day a certain feel of devotion and reverence.

I still love Lent. It still is a time for disciplined efforts and prayer. But I consider it special now because I see it as a focused time to try to better understand and surrender to God's perspective on things.

Jesus is God's perspective on things, and so in sharing with you these prayers from my journey, I have no greater desire than that they in some small way help bring you closer to him.

These prayers voice special regard for seniors but speak to the God who is the God of us all. May the graces of this holy season help you open up your life to God and to whatever blessings God wishes to bestow on you during this particular time of your life.

Dennis H. Ference

One

Conversion

∾

Even now, says the Lord,
return to me with all your heart,
with fasting, with weeping, and with
mourning;
rend your hearts and not your clothing.
Return to the Lord, your God.

JOEL 2:12,13a

God, I wish I could say that I have always been faithful to you over the many years of my life. I wish I could say that my focus on your truth has never been blurred by selfish wants and desires. I wish I could honestly say that my journey toward the goodness and beauty of your reign has never been sidetracked by fear, anxiety, and the struggle to make things come out my way.

But I come before you at the beginning of another Lenten season knowing that I can honestly say none of these things. I can only admit to myself and to you that your call to return to your paths is one that I must answer. Your call for a change of heart is one that I cannot ignore.

I accept the gritty ashes of Ash Wednesday on a body that reflects, like the ashes, the changes that come with the altering circumstances of time. But my need for you, I know, will never change. And so I ask you to help me recognize you as the center, goal, and meaning of my life. Bless this special time with your presence and your love. And, by the power of your grace, make me into more of the person you have created me to be.

Two

Something New

꩜

Neither is new wine put into old wine-skins; otherwise the skins burst, and the wine is spilled, and the skins are destroyed; but new wine is put into fresh wineskins, and so both are preserved.

MATTHEW 9:17

God, sometimes I feel like an old wine-skin. Sometimes I get so set and comfortable in the ways I've come to understand and do things. Then when I am faced with the need to consider new perspectives or changing circumstances, I become afraid that my world is on the verge of collapse. I suppose this is not an uncommon experience in later life when the diminishing flexibility of the body and mind can influence the flexibility of the spirit.

But God, you want me to grasp the fact that there is always something fresh and new about the life you offer. You always challenge me to let go of old expectations so that you can lead me into deeper meanings. And ultimately you always guide me to a way of living in which the only thing I totally depend on is you.

Help me, during this holy season, to allow you to make me into a fresh wineskin, ready for whatever new wine you wish to pour into me. Let me be eager for the surprise of its fragrance and the strength of its bite. Let me so love you that I can completely open myself to your plan for my life, no matter what changes I may have to make.

Three

Self-knowledge and Sin

∾

The Pharisees and their scribes were complaining to [Jesus'] disciples, saying, "Why do you eat and drink with tax collectors and sinners?" Jesus answered, "Those who are well have no need of a physician, but those who are sick; I have come to call not the righteous but sinners to repentance."

Luke 5:30-32

God, a good deal of my life has been taken up in discovering and rediscovering who I am. I have learned about my family heritage and how that plays into my identity. I have tried to understand my culture and how I am affected by its expressions. I have come to know myself as child, youth, adult, and now elder, and I have tried to come to terms with the significant realities each stage has introduced. I have worked to discover my strengths, gifts, and talents so that I could accept them and use them in spreading your love. I have made an effort to face my faults and weaknesses, my fears and defenses, and to become aware of how they interfere with my freedom.

As part of all this self-discovery, I have come to recognize that I am your blessed and loved child while at the same time a lost sheep and a sinner.

I suppose I'd rather not think of myself as a sinner, but I've seen enough of life and known enough people to understand that we're all sinners. I am comforted by

Scripture's assurances that admitting my sinfulness helps open my heart to your compassion and healing touch.

God, I know that I often try to hide from the truth, but I acknowledge to myself and to you this day, without excuses or my usual hedging, that I am indeed a sinner. Have mercy on me, God, and forgive me. Heal me and make me whole.

Four

God's Forgiveness

Then the father said to [the elder son], "Son, you are always with me, and all that is mine is yours. But we had to celebrate and rejoice, because this brother of yours was dead and has come to life; he was lost and has been found."

LUKE 15:31-32

God, I have sometimes been like the younger son in the Prodigal Son story—wasteful of your gifts, unscrupulous, and self-centered. Sometimes I have been like the elder son—self-righteous, rigid, and unforgiving. Neither way of behaving honors my dignity as your child.

Neither way leads to the peace and joy of your reign.

And yet, you want me to know that, like the father in this parable, you do not reject and condemn me for straying from what is right and good but continue to wait for my return home to you. You continue also to approach me with open arms, offering your compassion and forgiveness, always desiring to share with me the countless riches of your life.

Touch me deeply, O God, with your graciousness. Help me to return to your light whenever I foolishly step into the darkness. Let me open myself completely to your forgiveness without stubbornly holding on to guilt or shame. Let the reality of my weakness and sinfulness keep me humble and always deeply grateful for all that you do for me.

Five

Choice

❧

*I have set before you life and death,
blessings and curses. Choose life so that
you and your descendants may live, loving the LORD, your God, obeying...and
holding fast to [God].*

DEUTERONOMY 30:19,20a

God, as my years have multiplied, my
choices have diminished. Health
considerations, societal influences, felt
changes in interests and energy levels—
many things have narrowed the range of
my options.

And yet the most important choice has
always been and will always remain the

same until my last breath. It's the choice you set before me of life and death. It's the choice that reminds me so vividly of the deep respect you hold for the freedom you have given your children.

It does not matter if the death of this body is still years away or knocking at the door. I can always choose life over death by choosing to place my love for you above all else, by seeking till the very end to do your will as best as I can determine it, and by continuing to choose you again and again no matter how many times I may lose my way. This is the choice you so desire me to make. This is the choice for which you have created me. This is the choice that, with your help, I make this day.

Six

Fasting

❧

Is not this the fast that I choose:
to loose the bonds of injustice,
to undo the thongs of the yoke,
to let the oppressed go free,
and to break every yoke?
Is it not to share your bread with
the hungry,
and bring the homeless poor
into your house;
when you see the naked, to cover them,
and not to hide yourself from your
own kin?

ISAIAH 58:6-7

O God, the choice of life, of loving you, would seem to be an easy one. But frequently it is not. The truth is that I often struggle, confusing what is good with what is convenient or pleasurable. Every Lent your Church encourages the use of fasting, almsgiving, and prayer to point us in the right direction.

Aging has given me a new perspective on fasting. The experience of losses and diminishments that have come with these later years has suggested to me that fasting can perhaps most meaningfully be practiced now, not so much as a giving up but as a free and gracious letting go of what must pass in the changing circumstances of life. In this understanding, I recognize all as gift from you, a gift that is not meant to be held tightly or claimed as my own.

And so, as the one God and Creator of us all, you ask me especially to let go of the ways I try to selfishly separate myself from my brothers and sisters, the ways I isolate myself from their need.

Help me to understand that their hunger is my hunger, their nakedness is my nakedness, their oppression is my oppression. Help me to truly know that in loving and serving them, I am loving and serving you.

Seven

Almsgiving

~

Those who want to save their life will lose it, and those who lose their life for my sake will save it.

LUKE 9:24

G od, I've lived with myself for a very long time now. I've rightly had to be concerned about many things that affect my well-being—food, shelter, health care, finances. I've come to realize, however, that it's easy to get stuck in my own self-interests. It's easy to be overtaken by fear that there just isn't enough to go around.

Your Church encourages almsgiving as a way to put things in perspective, as a way of reminding us that we neither exist alone nor do we find our meaning in ourselves alone. It's a way of reminding us that we are simply stewards of the gifts you wish to bestow on all your children.

When you ask me to share my resources, you are asking me to share myself, to reach beyond my fears about loss of control and security that would keep me deaf and blind to the needs of those around me. You already know what I still must struggle to understand— excessive focus on self robs me of peace and freedom and joy. And life without peace and freedom and joy is hardly life at all.

God, I know that I must exercise prudence and wisdom in caring for my legitimate needs, but teach me to trust in you enough to lose my worries about myself so that I may experience the freedom of your reign and truly live.

Eight

Prayer

∾

Whenever you pray, do not be like the hypocrites; for they love to stand and pray in the synagogues and at the street corners, so that they may be seen by others.... Whenever you pray, go into your room and shut the door and pray to your Father who is in secret; and your Father who sees in secret will reward you.

MATTHEW 6:5,6

God, there is something wonderful and almost magical about presence. I have discovered that when people are really present with me in more than just a physical way, when they share themselves and not just their words, and when they truly listen to discover who I am, the moment together is charged and blessed with tremendous creative possibilities.

God, I have been praying to you almost as far back as I can remember. I have prayed formally and informally, in groups and alone, in the sacraments and in devotions, with many words and thoughts and with almost none. Sometimes I feel really connected to what I am doing, and sometimes I know that I am just going through the motions or performing a social function.

But in all my prayer, presence is what I do truly desire—the giving of my own presence to you and the experiencing of your presence deep in my heart. I've been praying long enough to know, however, that neither one of these always comes easily.

And so, as with everything else in my life, I need your help. Place in my heart such a desire for you in prayer that the desire itself consumes everything that would distract me from you. And in that desire, help me surrender my presence to you and open myself to every expression of your presence with which you may choose to grace me. Make this such a reality, my God, that my life itself may become more and more a prayer.

Nine

Temptation

❧

Jesus, full of the Holy Spirit, returned from the Jordan and was led by the Spirit in the wilderness, where for forty days he was tempted by the devil.

LUKE 4:1-2a

God, the liturgies of Lent remind me that no life's journey reaches its goal without passing through the desert of temptation. And the sands of that desert are so mixed with the soil of ordinary living that a day doesn't go by without an experience of temptation's lures and illusions.

Many of the temptations that trouble me today are as familiar as they are bothersome. The enticements of power, money, and regard continue to challenge my priorities and create questions about my values.

But the aging experience seems to have added, or at least intensified, certain temptations: I am tempted to take the wonder and freshness of your creation for granted; I am tempted to resent the ongoing reality of the cross and suffering in my life; I am tempted to block out the voice of the Spirit that calls me to change and grow no matter what my age.

Your Son experienced temptation in all its deceitful seductiveness and remained faithful to the truth of who he was and what he was sent to do. Strengthen me so that I too will remain faithful and become even more determined to serve you alone all the remaining days of my life.

Ten

Worship

❧

Our Father in heaven, hallowed be your name. Your kingdom come. Your will be done, on earth as it is in heaven.

MATTHEW 6:9-10

God, all that I do this Lenten season to open myself up to you I wish to do as worship. I want all of it to give praise to you and to speak of the recognition I have come to over these many years that my life is not my own. I want it to tell of my belief that my trust in you can overcome every one of the fears and temptations that work to destroy my peace and frustrate my freedom. I want it to sing of my growing acceptance of the truth that it is foolish to try to control all the circumstances of my life and look for security in anything but you. And I want it to give voice to my willingness to live truly connected to all my brothers and sisters rather than to stand apart and focus on myself alone.

But God, I know that even my strongest intentions often fail when they get mixed up with the messiness of this life. I know that pride and weakness are always around to distract and confuse. And so I humbly recognize that I must seek your help to create in this Lenten season the prayerful worship that I wish to give to you. Be with me, God, and assist me. Thank you, heavenly Father. Thank you. Hallowed be your name.

Eleven

Reconciliation

∾

When you are offering your gift at the altar, if you remember that your brother or sister has something against you, leave your gift there before the altar and go; first be reconciled to your brother or sister, and then come and offer your gift.

MATTHEW 5:23-24

God, you put such a priority on forgiveness and reconciliation, and yet I, your follower, continue to harbor old grudges. Some of them have been with me so long that they escape my awareness. And yet they eat away at my peace at the same time that new resentments sabotage my good intentions.

I suppose pride makes it difficult for me to let go of these personal hurts. True forgiveness can only come with a humble admission that I too am not perfect.

Regardless of my hesitation or reluctance, your direction remains the same— give priority to reconciliation.

And so I ask for your help to see the damage that my unwillingness to forgive does to me, and ultimately to the whole world. Give me the freedom that comes from reconciliation. Lead me to understand that the desire for oneness with you that you have placed in my heart includes the desire to share that oneness with all my brothers and sisters. Help me to recognize that desire. Inspire me to forgive others as you forgive me. Help me to be a person of love and peace.

Twelve

Discovery

❧

Make me to know your ways, O Lord;
teach me your paths.

Psalm 25:4

God, no matter how old I live to be or how wise I manage to become, I know that there will always be new lessons to learn and new things to experience. There simply is no way to exhaust the surprises of your creative hand.

And yet, I often experience a nagging feeling that you are calling me to go beyond my ordinary understanding of how to live my days and nights, to go deeper until my understanding and living of life reflect the very mystery of who you are and the holiness of your ways.

The Lenten season plunges me headlong into this journey of discovery and learning where I encounter once again such hard realities as suffering, the cross, and dying to self.

In all honesty, God, it is hard for me to open myself up to learn your paths and your ways when I know that what you wish to teach me points to the passion and death of Jesus. But even though I feel some hesitation about bringing myself before you as a student, I still believe that your ways are loving and meant to give me true peace and joy.

And so, my God, teach me and gently take me down the paths that lead unfailingly to you.

Thirteen

The Cross

*If any want to become my followers, let
them deny themselves and take up their
cross daily and follow me.*

LUKE 9:23

God, there was a time when I imagined designing my own cross, choosing the time and place I would lift it to my shoulder, and carrying it about for all to see. That was a time when I had an exaggerated sense of control over myself and life. I thought you were demanding nothing less than extraordinary heroics from me.

I eventually realized I didn't have that kind of control. I realized too that you are very much present in the simple and the ordinary. It became easier, then, to see that I don't have to go looking for crosses. I simply have to recognize them and face them as they come barging uninvited into my world each day.

And so, God, help me not to miss the importance of the cross in my life. Help me to truly understand that taking up my daily crosses in faithfulness to you marks me as a disciple of your Son.

In the death of a friend or loved one, the experience of chronic pain or disability, the demands of caring for a seriously ill spouse—in these and many other crosses, let me see a path to you. And then help me put my arms out in acceptance, surrender, and love for your Son, Jesus, who walks and suffers with me every step of the way.

Fourteen

Suffering

❧

The Son of Man must undergo great suffering, and be rejected by the elders, chief priests, and scribes, and be killed, and on the third day be raised.

LUKE 9:22

God, I don't understand why I sometimes expect my life to be free of suffering. Oh, I know in my head that I cannot escape suffering's touch, but in some corner of that place where fanciful imaginings survive, I continue to entertain the illusion that it might be possible to journey straight to Easter Sunday without passing through Good Friday. But the heart of the Lenten liturgies remind me year after year that there is only one road to glory, and it goes through suffering and death. And so I must come to terms with this challenging truth.

I want to think that if I pray hard enough, or work at it long enough, I can transform all my suffering into some experience that I find especially meaningful, encouraging, and maybe even beautiful. But your word reminds me that it is rather I that must be transformed by suffering, and my life given meaning and redemption by it.

And so, God, help me to understand that the answer to suffering for me lies not in searching out reasons and meanings. The answer lies in accepting my oneness with all of suffering humanity. The answer lies in uniting myself with Jesus in surrendering to your will.

Fifteen

Vulnerability

❧

I gave my back to those who struck me,
and my cheeks to those who pulled out
the beard;
I did not hide my face
from insult and spitting.
The Lord God helps me;
therefore I have not been disgraced.

Isaiah 50:6-7a

O God, there are so many different kinds of suffering in this life—the suffering of physical pain, of loss, of rejection, of fear and anxiety, of mistreatment by others. The list is long.

And as one ages, the experience of suffering seems to pick up a certain momentum as the body begins to fail, strength and energy wane, and losses begin to mount. Such realities are often accompanied by a feeling of uncertainty and a growing sense of vulnerability.

God, your Son knew all about vulnerability during the agony of his passion. He knew that he could not escape it if he was to fulfill his mission of love. He knew he had to consent to it and embrace it if he was to be truly one of us and our savior.

I may feel more vulnerable these days, but I have always been vulnerable. My youthful inexperience, in earlier times, simply blinded me to the full truth of the human condition.

God, in acknowledging and consenting to my vulnerability, I am dying to the self that secretly thinks it is the center of the universe. I am dying to the self that forgets how totally it depends on you.

But my vulnerability need not diminish my sense of worth. It need not overwhelm me with anxiety or make me feel any less loved by you.

Help me, God, to remember that my strength and dignity continues to come only from you, as it always has. And help me to remember that Jesus' sharing of our vulnerability brought us not defeat, but the greatest of victories and the fullness of life.

Sixteen

Strength through Weakness

∾

The stone that the builders rejected
  has become the cornerstone;
this was the Lord's doing,
  and it is amazing in our eyes.

MATTHEW 21:42 (SEE PSALM 118:22-23.)

God, why do I find it so hard to accept my vulnerability? I suppose because vulnerability is seen by the world as a form of weakness. And the values of the world encourage us to reject, hide, or deny weakness and imperfection.

But the whole life of Jesus makes me

pause to question the values that I tend to soak in from the world. Apparent failure, rejection, betrayal, the passion, the cross, the experience of abandonment—these all form an essential part of the legacy handed down in the story of Jesus. And that part of the legacy speaks decidedly of weakness rather than power.

The story ends in victory, but your Word affirms that there were no short-cuts to that victory. It also reminds me not to be so quick to reject any part of my experience that reflects weakness, defect, or imperfection. It may just be that what I want to reject is what you want to use to free me further for the life of your reign.

Help me, God, to look at the weak-nesses of these later years in a new way. Help me to see in them rich soil that can nourish your growing life within me. Help me to accept them as teachers and sign-posts that point to you.

Seventeen

Surrender and Faith

~

If our God whom we serve is able to deliver us from the furnace of blazing fire and out of your hand, O king, let him deliver us. But if not, be it known to you, O king, that we will not serve your gods and we will not worship the golden statue that you have set up.

Daniel 3:17-18

God, all stories in life do not have happy endings. The longer I live, the more I personally experience the reality that every illness will not be cured, every suffering cannot be avoided, every problem will not be resolved as I wish it to be.

In the face of the deepening of that realization at the very core of my being, you still ask me to surrender my life completely into your hands. Increasingly I know that faith cannot be simply a pious thought or sentiment. It must be a decision and a response.

I look to the life of your Son for inspiration and guidance, as I have all through this Lent. I look now especially to the agony in the garden. I consider Jesus' understanding of what was to come. I consider his anxiety and loneliness, the sweating of blood. I hear his words resonate as I think of my own past sufferings and those yet to come: "Father, if it is possible, let this cup pass from me; yet not what I want but what you want" (Matthew 26:39).

These are not words that are easy to contemplate. When I think of uttering them myself, I imagine them being born of pain and struggle and an almost desperate realization that the only real future there is for me comes from trusting you completely.

May I have the kind of trust in you that reflects the trust of your Son, Jesus. And may his words be in my heart and on my lips whenever I may become frightened or discouraged by the sufferings I must endure.

Eighteen

Love

❧

*[One scribe] asked him, "Which com-
mandment is the first of all?" Jesus
answered, "The first is, 'Hear, O Israel:
the Lord our God, the Lord is one; you
shall love the Lord your God with all
your heart, and with all your mind, and
with all your strength.' The second is
this, 'You shall love your neighbor as
yourself.'"*

MARK 12:28-31

G od, when I consider the purpose of
the Lenten season, I conclude that it
is largely to teach and nurture love. When
I contemplate the story of the life of Jesus,

and especially the story of his passion and death, I see that it is a story about love. When I wonder how you can be so forgiving, I conclude that it is because of your love. When I ask myself serious questions concerning the goal and meaning of my life, I find the most powerful and moving answers in love.

I think over my past, and I remember that love has healed me like nothing else could. Love has also inspired, united, compelled, and blessed me over and over like nothing else possibly could.

And love has drawn me to you because love is what you are all about. You are, in fact, love. Your Word has said it. I believe it to be true.

And so love is the goal before me always. It is the path. It is my guide. It is the response I wish to give to you now and every remaining moment of my life.

Teach me to love you and my brothers

and sisters without reservation. Teach me to love without fear. Teach me to love as you love me. Teach me, dear God, I beg you, teach me. Teach me to love.

Nineteen

Fulfillment

∾

The LORD will fulfill his purpose for me;
  your steadfast love, O LORD,
    endures forever.
Do not forsake the work of
  your hands.

PSALM 138:8

God, so often I experience my day with
a sense that I'm limping along in this
world, aware of a division and broken-
ness within me, urgently seeking to be
healed and brought to a wholeness and
peace that gives freedom and rest. Oh,
there have been many times when I have
felt snatches of that peace, but the

experience has always been temporary. I have been left with the returning need for a sense of completion and fulfillment.

I have attempted, my God, to pray this Lenten season by drawing my own life into the mystery of Jesus. I have attempted to see my journey in the light of his journey, to unite my sufferings with his.

I have seen through the grace of this time that I cannot come to completion and fulfillment by running from the hard realities of my life. I can only live my life trusting in you, consenting to your will, hoping in the sureness of your promises, and waiting for fulfillment of my journey according to the designs of your love. Thank you for the blessings of this season. They have helped me to be able to wait confidently for the blessings of the Easter season to come. Thank you for the sharing of your grace and wisdom. Thank you for loving me so much.